THE WRITER'S PLOT
JOURNAL

Turn Your Story Idea Into a Novel

Keely Brooke Keith

Edenbrooke
Press

Edenbrooke Press
Nashville, Tennessee

THE WRITER'S PLOT JOURNAL
Copyright 2018 Keely Brooke Keith

ISBN-13: 978-1728820323

Printed in the United States of America

To the sticky-note explosion in my office when I'm plotting.

On this journey…

Let this journal be a guide to help you turn your story idea into a novel or screenplay.

Your journey begins in Section One by journaling your story's basic elements: Who, What, When, Where, How, and Why. In Section Two, journal prompts will guide you in plotting your story using classic story structure but without being formulaic. Finally, Section Three contains blank pages for you to fill with story details, additional plot points, or scene ideas.

Though your completed story will flow logically for the reader, the plotting process often requires a lot of skipping back and forth. Extra journal pages are included after each question to give you plenty of space to come back to a particular point and journal more ideas, and several blank pages are included in Section Three of the journal.

It's easy to become distracted while journaling. Use the space in the wide margins to scribble thoughts that interrupt your journaling session. Once you get them out of the way, you can return your focus to the story.

As with every journal in the Guided Journals for Writers Series, when you feel resistance to a particular idea, consider it a spotlight for an issue you need to explore further on your journey.

This journal focuses on your story's plot. Though you will journal about your character and scene ideas in brief here, you'll want to use *The Writer's Scene Journal* and *The Writer's Character Journal* to expand your ideas.

Section One: The 6 Questions

"I keep six honest serving-men;
(They taught me all I knew)
Their names are What and Where and When
And How and Where and Who."

~THE ELEPHANT'S CHILD, Rudyard Kipling, *Just So Stories* (1902)

Who is in your story?

Name your protagonist and the supporting characters. What are their roles in your story? What do your main characters value most?

_____

_____

_____

_____

_____

_____

_____

_____

_____

_____

_____

_____

_____

_____

_____

_____

_____

_____

_____

_____

_____

_____

_____

The Who (continued)

_____

_____

_____

_____

_____

_____

_____

_____

_____

_____

_____

_____

_____

_____

_____

_____

_____

_____

_____

_____

_____

_____

_____

_____

_____

The Who (continued)

The Who (continued)

_____

_____

_____

_____

_____

_____

_____

_____

_____

_____

_____

_____

_____

_____

_____

_____

_____

_____

_____

_____

_____

_____

_____

_____

_____

_____

What is your protagonist's goal?

_____

_____

_____

_____

_____

_____

_____

_____

_____

_____

_____

_____

_____

_____

_____

_____

_____

_____

_____

_____

_____

_____

_____

_____

The What (continued)

The What (continued)

_____

_____

_____

_____

_____

_____

_____

_____

_____

_____

_____

_____

_____

_____

_____

_____

_____

_____

_____

_____

_____

_____

_____

_____

_____

_____

The What (continued)

How does your protagonist accomplish the goal?

_____

_____

_____

_____

_____

_____

_____

_____

_____

_____

_____

_____

_____

_____

_____

_____

_____

_____

_____

_____

_____

_____

_____

_____

_____

The How (continued)

The How (continued)

The How (continued)

_____

_____

_____

_____

_____

_____

_____

_____

_____

_____

_____

_____

_____

_____

_____

_____

_____

_____

_____

_____

_____

_____

_____

_____

_____

Why does your protagonist want to accomplish the goal?

Motivation comes from many sources but it's often rooted in a past wound
and the lie the character now believes about themselves, the world, or others.
What is your protagonist's motivation?

_____

_____

_____

_____

_____

_____

_____

_____

_____

_____

_____

_____

_____

_____

_____

_____

_____

_____

_____

_____

_____

_____

_____

The Why (continued)

_____

_____

_____

_____

_____

_____

_____

_____

_____

_____

_____

_____

_____

_____

_____

_____

_____

_____

_____

_____

_____

_____

_____

_____

The Why (continued)

The Why (continued)

When and where does your story take place?

A well-crafted setting can become a character in itself. Imagine you are in your setting and describe what you see, smell, hear, touch, and taste.

_____

_____

_____

_____

_____

_____

_____

_____

_____

_____

_____

_____

_____

_____

_____

_____

_____

_____

_____

_____

_____

_____

_____

_____

_____

_____

_____

_____

_____

_____

_____

_____

_____

_____

_____

_____

_____

_____

_____

_____

_____

_____

_____

_____

_____

_____

_____

The When and Where (continued)

The When and Where (continued)

Section Two: The Journey

Write your favorite quote about **journey** here:

_____

_____

_____

_____

'Twas the night before your story...

Imagine it is the evening before your story begins. Write a journal entry as if you are your protagonist. If your story has multiple point-of-view characters, use the following pages to write a journal entry for each of them.

_____

_____

_____

_____

_____

_____

_____

_____

_____

_____

_____

_____

_____

_____

_____

_____

_____

_____

_____

_____

_____

_____

_____

_____

Once upon a time…

Describe the opening scene of your story. Introduce your protagonist and give a sample of what life is like before the big event happens?

_____

_____

_____

_____

_____

_____

_____

_____

_____

_____

_____

_____

_____

_____

_____

_____

_____

_____

_____

_____

_____

_____

What is the theme of the story and how can you present it to the protagonist?

_____

_____

_____

_____

_____

_____

_____

_____

_____

_____

_____

_____

_____

_____

_____

_____

_____

_____

_____

_____

_____

_____

How can you introduce every A-story character and show their tics?

_____

_____

_____

_____

_____

_____

_____

_____

_____

_____

_____

_____

_____

_____

_____

_____

_____

_____

_____

_____

_____

_____

_____

_____

What inciting incident changes the protagonist's world?

_____

_____

_____

_____

_____

_____

_____

_____

_____

_____

_____

_____

_____

_____

_____

_____

_____

_____

_____

_____

_____

_____

What decision does your protagonist have to make? How will what your protagonist most values be at stake?

_____

_____

_____

_____

_____

_____

_____

_____

_____

_____

_____

_____

_____

_____

_____

_____

_____

_____

_____

_____

_____

_____

_____

How will your protagonist come to the decision to take the journey? What are the antagonistic forces and how can you show them? Describe your protagonist's inner quest as well as the outer challenge they must face.

_____

_____

_____

_____

_____

_____

_____

_____

_____

_____

_____

_____

_____

_____

_____

_____

_____

_____

_____

_____

_____

_____

Let the games begin…

Act II is the largest portion of most stories. Its rising action is a series of escalating complications that make it difficult for your protagonist to reach the goal. What is the first of at least three complications in your story?

_____

_____

_____

_____

_____

_____

_____

_____

_____

_____

_____

_____

_____

_____

_____

_____

_____

_____

_____

_____

What is the second of at least three complications in your story?

_____

_____

_____

_____

_____

_____

_____

_____

_____

_____

_____

_____

_____

_____

_____

_____

_____

_____

_____

_____

_____

_____

_____

What is the third of at least three complications in your story?

_____

_____

_____

_____

_____

_____

_____

_____

_____

_____

_____

_____

_____

_____

_____

_____

_____

_____

_____

_____

_____

_____

_____

_____

There is often a reversal at the midpoint of a story. New information or a new awareness empowers the protagonist or causes them to change their approach to the conflict. Sometimes the goal changes or the stakes are raised. What happens at the midpoint of your story?

_____

_____

_____

_____

_____

_____

_____

_____

_____

_____

_____

_____

_____

_____

_____

_____

_____

_____

_____

_____

_____

_____

_____

Act II generally ends with the protagonist beaten down. The old way of thinking dies. There is no hope. Describe the bleakest moment of your story.

_____

_____

_____

_____

_____

_____

_____

_____

_____

_____

_____

_____

_____

_____

_____

_____

_____

_____

_____

_____

_____

_____

_____

Don't look away…

Act III opens at the climax of the story.
What is your protagonist's super-strength and how do they summon it to overcome the obstacles and achieve the goal?

_____

_____

_____

_____

_____

_____

_____

_____

_____

_____

_____

_____

_____

_____

_____

_____

_____

_____

_____

_____

_____

In the falling action of the story, the consequences of the complications get resolved. How does your protagonist's inner journey and outer journey combine and reveal the solution?

_____

_____

_____

_____

_____

_____

_____

_____

_____

_____

_____

_____

_____

_____

_____

_____

_____

_____

_____

_____

_____

_____

_____

What closing scene(s) could show the change in your protagonist's life?

_____

_____

_____

_____

_____

_____

_____

_____

_____

_____

_____

_____

_____

_____

_____

_____

_____

_____

_____

_____

_____

_____

Section Three: More to the Story

This final section is for you to fill with story details, additional plot points, scene ideas, etc.

More Writing Resources

The Writer's Book Launch Journal: A Guided Book Marketing & Promotions Planner

Let *The Writer's Book Launch Journal* guide you through the marketing and promotional tasks every author should do to ensure a successful book launch. Filled with checklists of essential tasks, an abundance of publicity suggestions, and questions to personalize your promotions, *The Writer's Book Launch Journal* will lead you on the journey to a fun and fulfilling book launch.

The Writer's Purpose Journal: Discover Your Motivation For Writing

Do you want to write but don't know where to start? Are you halfway through your manuscript and feel blocked? Have you lost your enthusiasm for writing? Let *The Writer's Purpose Journal* guide you on a journey to rediscovering your purpose as a writer. Using questions to prompt soul-searching journal entries, *The Writer's Purpose Journal* will lead you through your beginnings as a writer, your influences, your goals, and your motivations to help you remove blocks and find fulfillment as a writer.

The Writer's Character Journal: Create a Varied Cast of Believable Characters

Let *The Writer's Character Journal* guide you through creating the varied cast of believable characters you'll need for your next novel. Using questions to prompt brainstorming, *The Writer's Character Journal* will help you flesh out your characters' pasts, quirks, relationships, strengths, fears, flaws, and more. Complete with a character index and numbering system for 18 characters.

The Writer's Scene Journal: Track Essential Elements To Craft Unforgettable Scenes

Let *The Writer's Scene Journal* guide you through crafting unforgettable scenes for your next novel. Using a list of essential elements, *The Writer's Scene Journal* will help you brainstorm your scenes' setting, plot, characters, sensory details, symbolism, and more. Complete with a scene index and numbering system for 45 scenes.

About The Author

Keely Brooke Keith writes inspirational frontier-style fiction with a futuristic twist, including *The Land Uncharted* (Shelf Unbound Notable Romance 2015) and *Aboard Providence* (2017 INSPY Awards Longlist).

Born in St. Joseph, Missouri, Keely was a tree-climbing, baseball-loving 80s kid. She grew up in a family who moved often, which fueled her dreams of faraway lands. When she isn't writing, Keely enjoys teaching home school lessons and playing bass guitar. Keely, her husband, and their daughter live on a hilltop south of Nashville, Tennessee.

Find Keely online at www.keelybrookekeith.com